DROPSHIPPING ON ETSY

Building a Successful Dropshipping Business on Etsy

The Wealth Publisher

CONTENT

INTRODUCTION

Welcome to "Dropshipping on Etsy: The Ultimate Guide to Building a Profitable Business". This book is designed to help you understand the ins and outs of dropshipping on Etsy and provide you with the tools you need to build a successful business.

If you're not familiar with dropshipping, it's a business model where you don't keep any inventory. Instead, you work with suppliers who ship products directly to your customers. This means you can start an online business without investing a lot of money upfront.

Etsy is a great platform for dropshipping because it has a large and active customer base that is interested in unique, handmade, and vintage items. However, dropshipping on Etsy can be challenging if you don't know where to start. That's why this book is here to help.

In this book, you'll learn:

- How to choose the right products to dropship on Etsy

- Where to find suppliers for your Etsy dropshipping business

- How to optimize your Etsy shop and product listings for maximum sales

- Etsy marketing strategies for dropshipping

- How to manage inventory and fulfil orders efficiently.

- How to manage customer service and returns with dropshipping on Etsy

- Legal considerations for Etsy dropshipping

By the end of this book, you'll have a solid understanding of dropshipping on Etsy and the tools you need to start and grow your own successful business. You'll be able to build a business that can generate passive income and help you achieve financial freedom.

Let's get started!

CHAPTER 1

Introduction to Dropshipping on Etsy

W elcome to the world of dropshipping on Etsy! If you're anything like me, you're probably tired of the daily grind of a 9-5 job and looking for a way to make some extra cash. Well, dropshipping on Etsy might just be the answer you're looking for!

Before we dive into the nitty-gritty details of how to dropship on Etsy, let's first understand what dropshipping is all about. In a nutshell, dropshipping is a business model where you don't hold any inventory. Instead, you work with suppliers who ship products directly to your customers.

Now, you might be thinking, "What? No inventory? How is that even possible?" Trust me, I had the same reaction when I first heard about dropshipping. But the beauty of this business model is that you don't have to worry about storing and managing inventory. All you need is a laptop, an internet connection, and some good suppliers.

So, why Etsy? Well, for starters, Etsy is one of the most popular online marketplaces in the world, with millions of buyers and sellers. But what makes Etsy unique is its focus on handmade, vintage, and unique items. This means that if you have a passion for creating or sourcing unique products, Etsy is the perfect platform for you.

But before you jump into dropshipping on Etsy, there are a few things you need to know. Let's take a look at some of the pros and cons of dropshipping on Etsy:

Pros:

Low startup costs: Since you don't need to invest in inventory upfront, you can start a dropshipping business on Etsy with very little money.

Flexibility: You can work from anywhere in the world as long as you have an internet connection.

Scalability: As your business grows, you can easily scale up by working with more suppliers and selling more products.

Passive income: Once you've set up your dropshipping business on Etsy, it can generate passive income for you.

Cons:

Competition: There's a lot of competition on Etsy, so it can be difficult to stand out from the crowd.

Limited control: Since you're working with suppliers, you don't have control over things like product quality or shipping times.

Fees: Etsy charges fees for listing products and processing payments, which can eat into your profits.

Legal considerations: You need to make sure you're complying with Etsy's policies and any applicable laws and regulations.

Now that you have a basic understanding of dropshipping on Etsy, it's time to dive deeper into the details. In the next chapter, we'll take a look at how to choose the right products to dropship on Etsy. But before we do that, let's do a quick exercise to get your creative juices flowing:

<u>Exercise:</u> Brainstorm a list of products you're passionate about and would like to sell on Etsy. Don't worry about whether they're practical or not – this is just to get your imagination going. Once you have a list, narrow it down to a few items that you think would be a good fit for dropshipping on Etsy.

CHAPTER 2

Choosing the Right Products to Dropship on Etsy

N ow that you've got your creative juices flowing, it's time to choose the right products to dropship on Etsy. This is an important step because it can make or break your dropshipping business. You want to choose products that are in demand and have a good profit margin. But how do you know what products to choose? Fear not, my friend, I've got you covered!

Here are some tips for choosing the right products to dropship on Etsy:

Research what's popular on Etsy:

One of the best ways to find out what's popular on Etsy is to browse the site and see what other sellers are selling. Look for items that have a lot of sales and good reviews. You can also use tools like EtsyRank or Marmalead to research popular keywords and trends on Etsy.

Look for products with a good profit margin:

You want to choose products that have a good profit margin so that you can make a decent profit. To calculate your profit margin, subtract the cost of the product from the selling price, and divide that by the selling price. Aim for a profit margin of at least 20%.

Choose products that are easy to ship:

Since you're dropshipping, you want to choose products that are easy to ship and won't cost a lot in shipping fees. Avoid products that are bulky or heavy, as they can be expensive to ship.

Consider your passions and interests:

As I mentioned in the previous chapter, it's important to choose products that you're passionate about. Not only will this make your business more enjoyable, but it will also give you a better understanding of your customers' needs and preferences.

Don't be afraid to test different products:

Don't put all your eggs in one basket. It's a good idea to test different products to see what sells well and what doesn't. This will help you identify profitable products and adjust your product line accordingly.

Now, let's do a quick exercise to help you choose the right products to dropship on Etsy:

Exercise: Choose three products that you're interested in and research them on Etsy. Look for products that have a high number of sales and good reviews, and calculate the profit margin for each product. Once you've done this, choose one product that you think would be a good fit for dropshipping on Etsy.

Congratulations, you've taken the first step towards building a profitable dropshipping business on Etsy! In the next chapter, we'll take a look at where to find suppliers for your Etsy dropshipping business. But before we do that, let's do one more exercise to get you thinking:

Exercise: Make a list of five potential suppliers for the product you chose in the previous exercise. Research each supplier and compare their prices, shipping times, and product quality. Choose one supplier that you think would be a good fit for your dropshipping business.

CHAPTER 3

Finding Suppliers for Your Etsy Dropshipping Business

Now that you've chosen your product, it's time to find a supplier for your Etsy dropshipping business. This can be a daunting task, but fear not, my friend, I'm here to guide you through it with some humour and helpful tips.

Here are some tips for finding suppliers for your Etsy dropshipping business:

Use a supplier directory: One of the easiest ways to find suppliers is to use a supplier directory like AliExpress or SaleHoo. These directories have a wide range of products and suppliers that you can choose from. They also have features like product reviews, supplier ratings, and shipping times to help you make informed decisions.

Contact manufacturers directly: Another option is to contact manufacturers directly. This can be a bit more time-consuming, but it allows you to negotiate prices and get better deals. You can find manufacturers by attending trade shows, searching online directories, or using platforms like Alibaba or Global Sources.

Check out Etsy Wholesale: Etsy Wholesale is a platform that connects Etsy sellers with wholesale suppliers. While it's not specifically for dropshipping, it can be a great resource for finding suppliers that offer unique and handmade products.

Consider local suppliers: If you prefer to work with local suppliers, consider attending craft fairs or reaching out to local artisans and makers. You can also search for suppliers on platforms like Etsy Local or Handmade at Amazon.

Ask for recommendations: Don't be afraid to ask other Etsy sellers for supplier recommendations. Join Etsy seller groups or forums and ask for advice. You can also reach out to successful Etsy dropshippers and ask for their supplier recommendations.

Now, let's do a quick exercise to help you find a supplier for your Etsy dropshipping business:

Exercise: Use a supplier directory like AliExpress or SaleHoo to search for suppliers for your chosen product. Compare prices, shipping times, and supplier ratings, and choose one supplier that you think would be a good fit for your business.

Congratulations, you've found a supplier for your Etsy dropshipping business! In the next chapter, we'll discuss how to optimize your Etsy shop and product listings to maximize sales. But first, let's do one more exercise to get you thinking:

Exercise: Take a look at your chosen product and analyze the competition on Etsy. Look at the top-selling shops and listings for similar products and take note of their titles, tags, descriptions, and photos. Use this information to optimize your own Etsy shop and product listings. Don't be afraid to get creative and stand out from the competition!

CHAPTER 4

Optimizing Your Etsy Shop and Product Listings for Maximum Sales

Congratulations on finding a supplier for your Etsy dropshipping business! Now it's time to optimize your Etsy shop and product listings for maximum sales. In this chapter, we'll cover some tips and tricks to help you stand out from the competition and attract more customers.

Use descriptive titles and tags:

Your titles and tags should accurately describe your product and include relevant keywords that customers might use to search for your product. Avoid using vague or misleading titles that might confuse customers or violate Etsy's policies.

Write compelling product descriptions:

Your product descriptions should be clear, concise, and highlight the unique features and benefits of your product. Use bullet points, headings, and bold text to make your descriptions easy to read and visually appealing.

Use high-quality photos:

Your product photos are the first thing customers will see when they visit your Etsy shop, so it's important to make a good impression. Use high-quality photos that showcase your product from multiple angles and in different settings. Consider hiring a professional photographer or investing in a good camera and lighting setup.

Offer competitive prices and free shipping:

Customers are more likely to buy from shops that offer competitive prices and free shipping. Do some research to find out what other Etsy sellers are charging for similar products and adjust your prices accordingly. You can also offer free shipping on orders over a certain amount to incentivize customers to buy more.

Respond promptly to customer inquiries and feedback:

Customer service is key to building a successful Etsy business. Respond promptly to customer inquiries and feedback, and strive to provide excellent customer service at all times. This will help you build a loyal customer base and attract positive reviews and feedback.

Keep your shop and listings up-to-date:
Regularly update your shop and listings with new products, promotions, and seasonal themes. This will help keep your shop fresh and interesting, and encourage customers to come back for more.

Now let's do a quick exercise to help you optimize your Etsy shop and product listings:

Exercise: Take a look at your current product listings and shop. Are your titles and tags accurate and descriptive? Are your product descriptions compelling and easy to read? Do your photos showcase your products in the best possible way? Make any necessary updates or improvements to your shop and listings based on the tips above.

Congratulations, you've optimized your Etsy shop and product listings for maximum sales! In the next chapter, we'll cover some marketing strategies to help you promote your Etsy business and attract more customers. But first, let's do one more exercise:

Exercise: Brainstorm some creative promotions or sales that you can offer to your Etsy customers. This could be a limited-time discount, a buy-one-get-one-free offer, or a free gift with purchase. Get creative and have fun with it!

CHAPTER 5

Etsy Marketing Strategies for Dropshipping

Now that you've optimized your Etsy shop and product listings, it's time to start promoting your business and attracting more customers. In this chapter, we'll cover some effective marketing strategies to help you reach your target audience and increase sales.

Utilize social media:

Social media is a powerful tool for promoting your Etsy business and connecting with potential customers. Create social media accounts for your business and share photos and updates about your products. Use hashtags to make your posts more discoverable and consider running paid ads on social media platforms to reach a wider audience.

Offer discounts and promotions:

Discounts and promotions are a great way to incentivize customers to buy from your Etsy shop. Consider offering a discount code to new customers or running a limited-time sale on select products. You can also offer free gifts with purchase or bundle deals to encourage customers to buy more.

Collaborate with influencers:

Influencer marketing is a popular way to promote products on social media. Reach out to influencers in your niche and offer to send them a free product in exchange for a social media post or review. This can help increase brand awareness and attract new customers to your Etsy shop.

Utilize Etsy advertising:

Etsy offers a variety of advertising options to help sellers promote their products on the platform. Consider running promoted listings, which will display your products at the top of search results for relevant keywords. You can also run Etsy ads, which will display your products on external websites and social media platforms.

Attend craft fairs and markets:

Attending craft fairs and markets is a great way to promote your Etsy business and connect with potential customers in person. Display your products and hand out business cards or flyers to attract new customers to your Etsy shop.

Now let's do a quick exercise to help you implement some of these marketing strategies:

Exercise: Choose one or two marketing strategies from the list above and implement them in your Etsy business. For example, you might create a social media account for your business and start sharing photos of your products. Or, you might offer a discount code to new customers to incentivize them to buy from your Etsy shop. Be creative and have fun with it!

Congratulations, you've learned some effective marketing strategies to promote your Etsy dropshipping business! In the next chapter, we'll cover some tips and tricks to help you manage your inventory and fulfill orders efficiently. But first, let's do one more exercise:

Exercise: Brainstorm some ideas for future promotions or collaborations that you can use to promote your Etsy business. This could be a holiday-themed sale, a collaboration with another Etsy seller, or a social media giveaway. Get creative and have fun with it!

CHAPTER 6

Managing Inventory and Fulfilling Orders Efficiently

A s your Etsy dropshipping business grows, it's important to have a solid system in place for managing your inventory and fulfilling orders efficiently. In this chapter, we'll cover some tips and tricks to help you streamline your processes and avoid common pitfalls.

Keep track of your inventory

It's important to have a clear understanding of your inventory levels at all times. Make sure to update your Etsy shop as soon as a product sells out or new stock arrives. You can also use inventory management software to help you track your stock levels and set up automatic reordering when inventory runs low.

Automate your order fulfillment:

Automating your order fulfillment process can save you time and reduce errors. You can use third-party software like Shipstation or Ordoro to automatically import orders from Etsy and print shipping labels with just a few clicks. You can also set up rules to automatically assign shipping carriers and shipping methods based on the customer's location and order details.

Communicate with your suppliers:

Good communication with your suppliers is key to ensuring that your orders are fulfilled on time and with high quality. Make sure to establish clear expectations and deadlines with your suppliers and keep them updated on any changes or issues with your orders. You can also consider using a supplier management tool like Sourcify or Alibaba to help you manage your supplier relationships more efficiently.

Offer tracking information to your customers:

Providing tracking information to your customers can help build trust and reduce customer inquiries about the status of their orders. Make sure to update your Etsy shop with tracking information as soon as it becomes available and consider sending automated email notifications to your customers when their orders ship.

Monitor your metrics:

Keeping track of key metrics like order volume, shipping times, and customer feedback can help you identify areas for improvement in your inventory management and order fulfillment processes. Use Etsy's built-in analytics tools to monitor your metrics and make adjustments as needed.

Now let's do a quick exercise to help you implement some of these tips:

Exercise: Review your current inventory management and order fulfillment processes and identify one or two areas where you can improve efficiency. For example, you might start using inventory management software to track your stock levels more accurately or automate your order fulfillment process to save time. Set a goal for yourself to implement these improvements within the next week.

Congratulations, you've learned some valuable tips and tricks for managing your inventory and fulfilling orders efficiently! In the next chapter, we'll cover some best practices for providing excellent customer service and handling customer inquiries and issues. But first, let's do one more exercise:

Exercise: Brainstorm some ideas for improving your customer service and handling customer inquiries more efficiently. This could be setting up an FAQ section on your Etsy shop, offering live chat support, or creating pre-written email templates to respond to common customer inquiries. Get creative and have fun with it!

CHAPTER 7

How to Manage Customer Service and Returns with Dropshipping on Etsy

P roviding excellent customer service is essential for any successful business, and dropshipping on Etsy is no exception. In this chapter, we'll cover some tips and best practices for managing customer inquiries and issues, as well as how to handle returns and refunds.

Be responsive and professional:

When it comes to customer service, it's important to be responsive and professional at all times. Respond promptly to customer inquiries and be courteous and helpful in your responses. Use proper grammar and spelling, and avoid using overly casual language or emojis, as this can come across as unprofessional.

Have a clear returns and refunds policy:

Having a clear and easy-to-understand returns and refunds policy can help prevent misunderstandings and build trust with your customers. Make sure to clearly outline your policy on your Etsy shop, including information on how to initiate a return or refund and any deadlines or restrictions.

Work with your suppliers to handle returns and exchanges:

When a customer requests a return or exchange, it's important to have a clear process in place for handling the transaction. Work with your suppliers to establish a process for handling returns and exchanges, including how to initiate a return, how to send the product back, and how refunds will be processed.

Use automated tools to handle customer inquiries:

Using automated tools like chatbots or pre-written email templates can help you handle customer inquiries more efficiently. You can set up a chatbot to answer common customer questions or create pre-written email templates for responding to common issues like shipping delays or product defects.

Monitor customer feedback and adjust your processes accordingly:

Monitoring customer feedback is essential for improving your customer service and overall business performance. Keep track of customer reviews and feedback on Etsy and other platforms, and use this information to make adjustments to your processes and policies as needed.

Now let's do a quick exercise to help you implement some of these tips:

Exercise: Review your current customer service processes and identify one or two areas where you can improve. For example, you might set up a chatbot to handle common customer inquiries or work with your suppliers to establish a clear process for handling returns and exchanges. Set a goal for yourself to implement these improvements within the next week.

Congratulations, you've learned some valuable tips and best practices for managing customer service and returns with dropshipping on Etsy! In the next chapter, we'll cover some advanced strategies for scaling your business and maximizing your profits. But first, let's do one more exercise:

Exercise: Brainstorm some ideas for improving your customer feedback and review management. This could include setting up an automated review request email, offering incentives for customers who leave reviews, or responding to negative reviews in a professional and helpful manner. Get creative and have fun with it!

CHAPTER 8

Scaling Your Etsy Dropshipping Business

C ongratulations on successfully starting your Etsy dropshipping business! Now that you've got the basics down, it's time to think about scaling your business to reach even greater levels of success. In this chapter, we'll cover some advanced strategies for growing your business and maximizing your profits.

Expand your product offerings:

One of the most effective ways to scale your Etsy dropshipping business is to expand your product offerings. This can help you reach new customers and increase your revenue streams. Look for new and trending products that align with your brand and target audience, and work with your suppliers to add them to your product lineup.

Automate your processes:

As your business grows, it can become increasingly difficult to manage all of the moving parts. Automating your processes can help you streamline your operations and save time and resources. Look for tools and software that can help you automate tasks like order fulfillment, inventory management, and customer service.

Optimize your pricing strategy:

Pricing is a critical component of your business strategy, and it's important to regularly review and optimize your pricing to ensure that you're maximizing your profits. Consider using dynamic pricing strategies like tiered pricing or time-limited discounts to encourage customers to make a purchase.

Focus on customer retention:

Acquiring new customers is important, but retaining existing customers can be even more valuable for your business. Focus on providing excellent customer service, creating a loyalty program, or offering exclusive discounts or promotions for repeat customers.

Consider expanding to other marketplaces:

While Etsy is a great platform for dropshipping, there are other marketplaces and platforms that can offer even greater opportunities for growth. Consider expanding your business to other platforms like Amazon, eBay, or Shopify to reach new customers and diversify your revenue streams.

Now let's do a quick exercise to help you implement some of these tips:

Exercise: Identify one or two areas where you can improve your business operations to help you scale your business. For example, you might consider adding new products to your lineup or automating your order fulfillment process. Set a goal for yourself to implement these improvements within the next month.

Congratulations, you've learned some valuable tips and strategies for scaling your Etsy dropshipping business! By implementing these strategies and continually innovating and optimizing your business operations, you can achieve even greater levels of success and financial freedom.

CHAPTER 9

Legal Considerations for Etsy Dropshipping

H ey there, dropshippers! While it's easy to get caught up in the excitement of starting and growing your Etsy dropshipping business, it's important to remember that there are legal considerations that you need to keep in mind. In this chapter, we'll go over some of the key legal considerations you should be aware of when dropshipping on Etsy.

Business Structure:

One of the first things you need to consider when starting your Etsy dropshipping business is your business structure. This refers to how your business is legally organized, such as a sole proprietorship, partnership, or LLC. Each structure has its own benefits and drawbacks, so it's important to do your research and choose the one that best fits your needs.

Business Licenses and Permits:

Depending on where you live and the type of products you sell, you may need to obtain certain licenses and permits to operate your Etsy dropshipping business legally. Check with your local and state government to find out what licenses and permits you need, and make sure to keep them up-to-date.

Taxation:

Sales tax can be a confusing and complicated topic for many dropshippers. The rules and regulations around sales tax vary depending on where you live and where your customers are located. Make sure to do your research and consult with a tax professional to ensure that you're collecting and remitting the appropriate amount of sales tax.

Intellectual Property:

When dropshipping on Etsy, it's important to be aware of intellectual property laws and regulations. This includes trademarks, copyrights, and patents. Make sure that you have the appropriate rights to use any images or logos on your products, and avoid using any trademarks or copyrighted materials without permission.

Consumer Protection:

As a business owner, you have a responsibility to protect your customers from fraud and other illegal activities. Make sure to be transparent about your business practices, including your refund and return policies, and always strive to provide excellent customer service.

Now, let's do a quick exercise to help you stay on top of these legal considerations:

Exercise: Take some time to research and familiarize yourself with the legal requirements for operating a dropshipping business on Etsy in your area. Make a checklist of the licenses, permits, and taxes you need to comply with, and create a plan to stay on top of them.

Congratulations, you've learned some valuable legal considerations for operating your Etsy dropshipping business! By staying on top of these requirements and working with legal and tax professionals as needed, you can ensure that your business operates legally and ethically.

CHAPTER 10

Frequently Asked Questions about Dropshipping on Etsy

C ongratulations on making it this far in your dropshipping journey on Etsy! By now, you should have a pretty good grasp of what dropshipping is, how it works on Etsy, and how you can get started.

But as with any new venture, there are always going to be questions that pop up along the way. In this final chapter, we'll address some of the most frequently asked questions about dropshipping on Etsy.

Q: Can I dropship products from AliExpress on Etsy?

A: Yes, you can. In fact, AliExpress is one of the most popular sources for dropshippers on Etsy. However, you'll need to make sure that the products you're selling meet Etsy's guidelines and standards.

Q: How much money can I make dropshipping on Etsy?

A: That really depends on a variety of factors, such as the products you're selling, your profit margins, your marketing strategy, and more. Some dropshippers on Etsy are able to make a full-time income, while others use it as a side hustle to supplement their existing income.

Q: Do I need to have a business license to dropship on Etsy?

A: That depends on your location and the laws in your area. In general, if you're running a business, you'll need to have a business license. Check with your local government to find out what the requirements are for your area.

Q: *Do I need to keep inventory if I'm dropshipping on Etsy?*

A: No, that's the beauty of dropshipping! Your supplier will handle all of the inventory and shipping for you.

Q: *Can I offer free shipping on my Etsy dropshipping products?*
A: Yes, you can. However, you'll need to factor in the cost of shipping when setting your prices to ensure that you're still making a profit.

Q: *What happens if my supplier runs out of stock?*

A: Ideally, your supplier should notify you ahead of time if they're running low on stock. If they do run out, you'll need to find a new supplier or temporarily remove the product from your Etsy shop.

Q: *How do I handle returns and refunds with dropshipping?*

A: This will vary depending on your supplier's policies. Make sure you understand their return and refund policies before you start selling their products on Etsy. In general, you'll need to coordinate with your supplier to handle any returns or refunds.

Q: *What if my customers have questions or concerns about their orders?*

A: As the seller, it's your responsibility to provide excellent customer service. Make sure you're available to answer any questions or concerns your customers may have, and work with your supplier to resolve any issues that may arise.

Q: *Is dropshipping on Etsy a sustainable business model?*

A: Like any business model, dropshipping on Etsy has its pros and cons. However, many dropshippers on Etsy have been able to build successful and sustainable businesses using this model.

Q: Do I need to be an expert in marketing to be successful at dropshipping on Etsy?

A: No, but having a solid understanding of marketing will certainly help you succeed. Take the time to learn about SEO, social media marketing, email marketing, and other marketing strategies that can help you promote your products and reach more customers.

CONCLUSION

Congratulations! You've made it to the end of the book. By now, you should have a good understanding of dropshipping on Etsy and how it can help you achieve financial freedom.

I hope that you found this book informative, engaging, and humorous. It was my intention to provide you with practical advice and actionable steps that you can take to start and grow your own Etsy dropshipping business.

And with that, we've come to the end of our dropshipping on Etsy journey! We hope this book has provided you with valuable insights and practical tips for building a successful Etsy dropshipping business. Remember to always be learning, experimenting, and adapting as you go.

Before I sign off, I'd like to leave you with a few key takeaways:

Etsy dropshipping is a great way to start an online business with little investment and risk.

You need to choose the right products, find reliable suppliers, and optimise your Etsy shop and product listings to maximise sales.

Marketing and customer service are crucial for the success of your Etsy dropshipping business.

Always keep legal considerations in mind and be transparent with your customers.

Scaling your Etsy dropshipping business requires hard work and dedication, but it can lead to great rewards.

Remember, the journey to financial freedom is not easy, but it is achievable. With the right mindset, strategies, and support, you can create a successful Etsy dropshipping business that can provide you with the financial stability and freedom you desire.

Thank you for choosing this book and good luck on your dropshipping journey!

www.ingramcontent.com/pod-product-compliance
Lightning Source LLC
Chambersburg PA
CBHW071117220526
45467CB00004B/1927